20TH CENTURY Pop Culture

The Early Years–1949

Produced by Carlton Books

20 Mortimer Street

London, W1N 7RD

Text and design copyright © Carlton Books Limited 1999/2000

First published in hardback edition in 2001 by Chelsea House Publishers, a subsidiary of

Haights Cross Communications. Printed and bound in Dubai.

First Printing

1 3 5 7 8 6 4 2

The Chelsea House World Wide Web address is http://www.chelseahouse.com

Library of Congress Cataloging-in-Publication Data applied for

The Early Years –1949   ISBN: 0-7910-6084-5

The 50s   ISBN: 0-7910-6085-3

The 60s   ISBN: 0-7910-6086-1

The 70s   ISBN: 0-7910-6087-X

The 80s   ISBN: 0-7910-6088-8

The 90s   ISBN: 0-7910-6089-6

20TH CENTURY Pop Culture

The Early Years–1949

Dan Epstein

Chelsea House Publishers

Philadelphia

20TH CENTURY

Pop Culture

Contents

1900 1945

1900: A Century Begins

What a difference a century makes. The intrepid time-traveler from 1999 would barely recognize the America of 1900— a country where most people worked over sixty hours a week, the average summer wardrobe provided more body coverage than today's winter sportswear, and music lovers had to visit special "phonograph parlors" in order to hear the latest recordings. Expensive and generally unreliable, the few automobiles on the road (only four thousand were even manufactured in 1900) tended to belong to wealthy Americans; the rest relied upon ten million bicycles and eighteen million mules and horses to take them through the nation's unpaved streets. Not exactly the stuff of MTV programming, is it?

And yet, some things haven't changed much. In 1900, the US military was involved in a controversial conflict in a far-off land—though this one was taking place in the Philippines, as opposed to Kosovo. Then, as now, there were those who sought to impose their sense of morality upon their fellow citizens; prohibition crusader **Carry Nation** led her volunteers through the state of Kansas, using hatchets to destroy saloons and other businesses that sold liquor. And, while they weren't called "hate crimes" back then, anti-minority violence was still quite commonplace, with one hundred and five blacks reportedly lynched during that year.

On a lighter note, college football, boxing, and professional baseball were as popular as they are today (even more so, in the case of the latter two), and the lucky patron who frequented the Louis Lunch Counter in New Haven, Connecticut could partake of a new sandwich called the **hamburger**. The establishment's spartan beef-patty-on-toast presentation might well perplex the modern-day Big Mac aficionado, however; hamburger buns wouldn't be popularized until the St. Louis World's Fair of 1903, and it would take another three decades for someone to come up with the idea of dressing a burger with a slice of cheese.

1901–1914: A Brave New Era

In many ways, the new American century didn't really begin until September 14, 1901, when President William McKinley died of complications from a gunshot wound inflicted by anarchist Leon Czolgosz. A dour, conservative politician with ties to big business and decidedly "imperialist" leanings, McKinley was every inch a late-nineteenth-century president. **Theodore "Teddy" Roosevelt**, the man who succeeded him, was a different animal entirely; a charismatic renaissance man with "war hero," "state governor," "cowboy," and "historian" already on his resumé, his boundless energy and progressive politics were a perfect match for the optimistic young country.

Now that the US had finally extricated itself from the rebellion in the Philippines (itself a by-product of the recent Spanish-American War), Roosevelt was free to concentrate on strengthening the country by preserving its natural resources, busting big-business "trusts," and trying to improve race relations

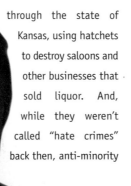

■ Theodore "Teddy" Roosevelt— a new leader for a new age

(though many Americans protested when he invited black educator Booker T Washington to a White House dinner, Roosevelt stood firm). He also appointed a commission to investigate the country's meat industry, after Upton Sinclair's harrowing novel *The Jungle* (1906) exposed the terrible working conditions in meat-packing plants, as well as the fact that the beef sent to market often came from diseased cattle. The ensuing probe led to the government's passage of the Pure Food and Drug and Meat Inspection acts, which enforced new standards of cleanliness for the country's food manufacturers.

Beverage companies were also falling under a fair amount of scrutiny at this time; in 1903, the **Coca-Cola** Company was forced to remove unprocessed coca leaves from its recipe, after several newspapers and various concerned citizens began to rail against the (actually rather minuscule) quantity of cocaine contained in the soft drink. Coke had already been around for two decades, but many of the products we take for granted today were actually introduced or invented during this period. **Kellogg's Corn Flakes** hit the market in 1902; over a hundred thousand pounds of the cereal were sold during its first year on the shelves. New Jersey ice cream salesman Italio Marcioni patented the ice-cream cone in 1903; George Schmidt and Fred Osius of Racine, Wisconsin introduced the first electric milkshake mixer in 1904; Gennaro Lombardi opened the country's first pizzeria in New York's Little Italy in

1905; and in 1906, vendor Harry Mosley Stevens began wrapping sausages with buns at New York's Polo Grounds ballpark, thus establishing the still-intact connection between baseball and **hot dogs**.

Of course, the American spirit of invention spread far beyond the realm of foodstuffs. In 1907, the Ideal Novelty Company sold a million of their new "teddy bears," stuffed animals inspired by the then-popular (and probably apocryphal) tale of a friendly encounter between President Roosevelt and an orphaned bear cub.

■ The Model "T" Ford—the car that changed the world.

In 1913, Gideon Sundback, a Swedish engineer from Hoboken, New Jersey, patented the **zipper** fastener; a year later, New York debutante Mary Phelps Jacob patented the first elasticized, backless brassiere. And one certainly mustn't forget brothers Orville and Wilbur Wright, who made aviation history by flying their home-made, 750-lb aircraft along the beach at Kitty Hawk, North Carolina. The date was December 17, 1903, and it marked the first actual flight by a heavier-than-air vehicle.

Advances were also coming fast and furious in the automotive field. In 1900, Packard's Model C became the first car to be fitted with a steering wheel, a positively futuristic device compared to the tillers then in use for other models. The Olds Company of Detroit, Michigan established the first mass-production automobile factory the same year, but it was **Henry Ford** who really popularized the concept. Ford's Model T had sold well

from its 1908 debut, but the company's 1913 switch to mass production enabled Ford to crank out a thousand cars a day at remarkably affordable prices, resulting in the sales of nearly sixteen million Model T's between 1908 and 1927. Available "in any color you like, as long as it's black," the **Model T** proved such a success that most of the country's other manufacturers began producing their own front-engine, gas-powered (many earlier cars were powered by steam) models that looked remarkably like Ford's "Tin Lizzie." Oft-imitated but never quite duplicated, the reliable and wallet-friendly Model T almost single-handedly turned America into a nation of car drivers.

Thomas Edison applied similar mass-production techniques to his phonograph cylinders, but the cumbersome format was ultimately destined to fail. His chief competitor, the Victor Talking Machine Company, made phonographs (popularly known as **"Victrolas"**) which played flat discs, a far more convenient format. As a result, Americans who used to gather around the family piano for

■ Kellogg's Corn Flakes

musical entertainment (wealthier homes often boasted automated "player" pianos) were starting to buy more records than sheet music. In 1905, Arthur Collins' "The Preacher And The Bear" (one of the many racist "coon" songs then in vogue) became the first record to sell a million copies. The ragtime music of Jelly Roll Morton became quite popular during this period, but it was four-part "**barbershop**" harmony singing that really defined the music of the era. One of the better-known barbershop quartets was the Haydn Quartet, whose renditions of "Sweet Adeline" (1904) and "By The Light Of The Silvery Moon" (1910) could be heard emanating from Victrolas everywhere.

The film industry grew by leaps and bounds during this period, though—like baseball, vaudeville, and burlesque shows—moving pictures were generally considered a vulgar and disreputable pastime. Of course, such snobbery didn't exactly hinder the proliferation of **nickelodeons** (which numbered between eight and ten thousand by 1908), or keep the hundreds of thousands of regular nickelodeon customers from paying five cents to view such three-minute shorts as *Gertie the Dinosaur* (a 1909 animated film featuring the drawings of newspaper cartoonist Winsor McCay), *In Old Kentucky* (a 1909 drama starring Mary Pickford, one of the industry's first stars, and directed by the tremendously prolific and influential DW Griffith), or the many slapstick "Keystone Cops" comedies of director Mack Sennett.

"Cultivated" persons tended to prefer the theater, flocking to see such stage productions as Florenz Zeigfield's *Ziegfield Follies* (featuring

"the most beautiful girls in the world"), George M Cohan's *Forty-Five Minutes from Broadway*, and George Broadhurst's melodramatic *Bought and Paid For*. The influence of the period's theatergoers can best be gauged by the fact that, while thousands of American coal miners died in mine explosions and cave-ins during the first decade of the century, the demands for improved mine safety paled next to the outcry for new theater building codes that followed Chicago's Iroquois Theater fire, which killed 588 patrons in 1903.

Other significant disasters of the period included the 1912 sinking of the "unsinkable" British ocean liner *Titanic*, which killed nearly 1500 British and American passengers, and the massive **San Francisco earthquake** of 1906, which (along with the fire that followed) killed two and a half thousand San Franciscans, left three hundred thousand homeless, and destroyed over twenty-eight thousand of the city's buildings. Less massively cataclysmic, though far more preventable, was the 1911 fire at New York City's Triangle Shirtwaist Company, which killed one hundred and forty-six female garment workers—most of whom could have been saved had the building been equipped with fire escapes and emergency exits.

With the age of the "skyscraper" already in full swing, the substantial revisions of the city's building code that followed the Triangle Shirtwaist tragedy came not a moment too soon. On one evening in 1913, President Woodrow Wilson pressed a button that illuminated Manhattan's newly-completed **Woolworth Building** with eighty thousand light-bulbs.

At sixty stories and 792 feet, the gothic structure was now the world's tallest building, besting its closest competitor—1908's Metropolitan Life Tower, located several miles uptown—by almost a hundred feet. It would be nearly two decades before anybody built one higher.

1915–1929: A World War And "The Roaring Twenties"

As "The Great War" raged in Europe, debate raged at home about whether

Higher and higher—the Woolworth Building scrapes the sky in New York City.

or not the United States should enter the fray. The Peerless Quartet's "I Didn't Raise My Boy To Be A Soldier," a song with unabashedly pacifist sentiments, was one of the top sellers of 1915, despite the fact that one hundred and twenty-three Americans had been killed in May when the British steamship *Lusitania* was sunk by a German submarine.

Still, while President Wilson's 1916 re-election campaign used "**He Kept**

Us Out Of The War" as its slogan, both Wilson and the American people knew that it would only be a matter of time before US soldiers joined their British and French counterparts in the trenches along the Western Front. By June 26, 1917, when the first US troops landed in France, anti-German sentiment had built to the point where Tin Pan Alley songwriters were making piles of money cranking out ditties with titles like "We're All Going Calling On The Kaiser," "When I Send You A Picture Of Berlin," and "We Don't Want The Bacon (What We Want Is A Piece Of The Rhine)." Most popular of all was George M Cohan's "**Over There**," which spent most of the year at the top of the sales charts, thanks to an appropriately brash rendition by The American Quartet.

Though World War One was far less damaging to the United States than to its allies, the country hardly emerged unscathed; 116,708 American soldiers died in the war (more than half of them from disease), while another 204,002 returned wounded. The lingering memories of the war's horrors and privations (and of the influenza epidemic that killed over four hundred thousand Americans in the autumn of 1918) manifested themselves in both the harsh realism of authors like Ernest Hemingway, F Scott Fitzgerald, and John Dos Passos, and the general public's almost nihilistic desire to party as if there was no tomorrow.

It was in this environment that **jazz** music, once strictly the province of Kansas City and New Orleans brothels, began to flourish nationally, as the "hot" music of bandleaders like Paul Whiteman and Louis Armstrong—now coming into homes via a new invention called radio—tapped into the pent-up energies of the populace. In 1923, the Broadway musical *Runnin' Wild* helped turn the **Charleston** into the latest dance craze; as with the short hemlines of the new "flapper" fashions, the energetic dance was emblematic of the era's shift to a sexier, more carefree mood.

Of course, there was the slight matter of **Prohibition** to contend with. On January 29, 1919, the US Congress ratified the Eighteenth Amendment to the Constitution, outlawing the manufacture, sale, and transportation of alcohol throughout the entire country. Long considered a "noble experiment" by its many supporters, Prohibition had already taken hold in twenty-four states; but as of January 16, 1920, when the Amendment took effect, it was now impossible to purchase a drop of liquor anywhere in the country—legally, that is. While the rest of the economy was feeling the negative effects of the postwar manufacturing slowdown, business was absolutely booming for bootleggers. Every town had at least one "**speakeasy**," a clandestine saloon that served booze, and rare was the gentleman who travelled without his hip flask. Stories abounded about people who'd been blinded or sickened by drinking homemade "bathtub gin," but demand for the stuff continued to override any medical, moral, or legal concerns.

■ **Al Capone (1899–1947) with US Marshal Laubenheimer.**

As Chicago gangster **Al Capone** put it, "When I sell liquor, it's bootlegging. When my patrons serve it on silver trays on Lake Shore Drive, it's hospitality."

In short, the "noble experiment" proved a tremendous failure. Over the course of the decade, federal and state officials arrested an estimated half-million people for manufacturing or importing alcohol, but the illegal booze continued to flow. If anything, Prohibition created a bigger problem than the one it sought to eradicate—namely, the rise of organized crime, which was primarily financed by bootlegging profits. The hub of gangland activity was Chicago, where gang warfare killed over six hundred people during the 1920s. The most famous gang-related incident of the era took place on February 14, 1929: "**The St Valentine's Day Massacre**," in which seven members of Bugs Moran's gang were gunned down in a Chicago warehouse. Though Al Capone was widely believed to have ordered the hit, police lacked enough evidence to bring him in. Capone's reign of terror was effectively ended three months later, when he was sentenced to a year in prison for carrying a concealed weapon. Tax

■ **Footloose and fancy free— flappers scale the heights**

evasion charges—and the ravages of syphillis—would keep "Scarface" out of action for the remainder of his life.

Charles Lindbergh became a national hero in 1927, when he piloted his "*Spirit of St Louis*" to Paris in the first solo flight across the Atlantic, but the era seemed to produce as many infamous figures as exemplary ones. Among the notable folks running afoul of the law were the Chicago White Sox, whose starting lineup was accused of taking bribes to intentionally lose the 1919 World Series. The players were eventually acquitted, but it took several years (and the ascendance of colorful slugger Babe Ruth, who hit a record 60 home runs in 1927) for professional baseball to completely lose the taint of "**The Black Sox Scandal.**" Also beset by scandal was President Warren G. Harding, whose administration was positively riddled by corruption; his death on August 2, 1923 of a pulmonary embolism ¯some have alleged that he was poisoned—was probably the only thing that saved him from being thrown out of office.

Perhaps the most notorious scandal of the era involved comedic actor **Roscoe "Fatty" Arbuckle**, whose star turns in films like *His Wedding Night* and *The Life of the Party* had, by 1921, earned him a million-dollar-a-year contract with Paramount Studios. The film industry had grown substantially since relocating from the East Coast in the years before the First World War, but many Americans perceived Hollywood as nothing less than a seething pit of godless iniquity. Therefore, when Arbuckle was accused of raping and mortally injuring aspiring actress Virginia Rappe, it only confirmed the

Charlie Chaplin in "The Goldrush".

worst suspicions of the country's moral watchdogs. After two deadlocked trials, a third found Arbuckle not guilty, but it would be another decade before the rotund comic again found work in the industry.

DW Griffith, the most important director of the era, was another film great who found himself *persona non grata* in Hollywood, albeit for reasons far less tawdry. His 1915 epic *Birth of a Nation* was a box-office smash—even though it drew criticism for its sympathetic portrayal of the Ku Klux Klan, a late-nineteenth-century Southern hate group then experiencing a revival—but the multiple plot lines of his next film, 1916's *Intolerance*, left audiences scratching their heads. Griffith regained some of his commercial

momentum in 1919 with *Broken Blossoms*, a lovely film for United Artists, the new company he formed with popular stars Charlie Chaplin (already famous for his "Little Tramp" character), Mary Pickford, and Douglas Fairbanks; but for all his formidable artistry, the director's propensity for going over budget—and his inability to tailor his filmmaking style to the tastes of 1920s audiences— completely alienated him from his colleagues.

Along with Chaplin, Pickford, and Fairbanks, other leading lights of the "golden age of silent film" included Western stars William S Hart and Tom Mix, screen beauties Clara Bow and Norma Talmadge, acrobatic comedians Buster Keaton and Harold Lloyd, canine hero Rin Tin Tin, horror film star Lon Chaney (whose deft use of makeup earned him the nickname "Man of a Thousand Faces") and

romantic lead Rudolph Valentino, whose premature death in 1926 set off a wave of worldwide hysteria.

For the country, the period between 1922 and 1929 brought an unprecedented surge of prosperity; for the motion-picture industry, the attendant leap in box-office receipts resulted in lavish movie theaters—like the Roxy in New York City, and Grauman's Chinese in Hollywood—and tremendous advances in film technology. Though Charlie Chaplin was heard to opine that "moving pictures need sound as much as Beethoven symphonies need lyrics," the days of silent film were definitely numbered.

The Jazz Singer, which premiered in October of 1927, caused a sensation with its synchronized sound effects, talking sequences, and songs sung by recording star Al Jolson. The following year saw every major film studio hop on the sound bandwagon; some of the more notable early efforts included Warner Bros.' *Lights of New York* (helpfully billed as "100 percent all-talking") and Walt Disney's *Steamboat Willie*, the first animated sound film, which also starred an early version of Mickey Mouse. Unfortunately, the advent of "**talkies**" also spelled early retirement for many silent stars—including Norma Talmadge, John Gilbert, and Marie Prevost—whose speaking voices failed to live up to the personas they'd created for the silver screen.

Like the silent films themselves, the prosperity and *joie de vivre* that characterized the "Roaring Twenties" would not live to see the end of the decade. Stock prices had reached an all-time high on September 3, 1929, but it simply couldn't last; stocks soon began a drastic decline, with the biggest crash coming on October 29, better known as "**Black Tuesday**." Within weeks, holdings on the New York Stock Exchange had dropped twenty-six million dollars, and the country (indeed, much of the world) would spend the next decade trying to recover. The Great Depression was underway.

1930–1944: The Great Depression And Another Global Conflict

"Happy Days Are Here Again" went the most popular song of 1930, but for most Depression-era Americans, the sentiment strictly amounted to wishful thinking. "Brother Can You Spare A Dime," a 1932 hit for both Bing Crosby and Rudy Vallee, was probably more to the point: By October of 1930, four and a half million Americans were unemployed; two months later, New

York City's Bank of the United States suddenly went out of business, leaving four hundred thousand depositors empty-handed, and "bank panics"—wherein customers ran to withdraw their balances before their banks could close on them—soon became commonplace.

The Depression drove most of Detroit's auto makers out of business, and basically did the same for **Herbert Hoover**. Hoover, elected President in 1928 at the height of American prosperity, had responded to the country's economic plight by laying plans for government-funded public works programs, as well as voluntarily taking a twenty-percent cut in pay; but in the minds of voters—thirteen million of whom were unemployed by late 1932—Hoover was synonymous with the hard times that had recently come to pass. As a result, Franklin Delano Roosevelt, the former governor of New York, beat Hoover by a landslide in the 1932 elections. **FDR**'s runaway victory came as something of a surprise to the Hoover camp, who wrongly assumed that the American public would never elect a paraplegic to the country's highest office. In fact, Roosevelt's indomitable optimism, which had served him so well during his initial recovery from polio, was probably even more attractive to the voters of the day than his much-vaunted "New Deal" platform.

FDR's other major asset was his mellifluous speaking voice, which seemed tailor-made for the medium of radio. A few days after his initial inauguration, Roosevelt began delivering regular radio addresses to the nation. These genial "**fireside chats**," as he liked to call them, did a lot to improve the morale of the

country during the lean times; they also kept him in good standing with the voters—even when the country's newspapers called for his head, as they often did during the 1930s.

Of course, Roosevelt's "fireside chats" weren't the only thing Americans were listening to. Since 1922, when a system for parceling out wavelengths was first established, **the radio industry** had grown rapidly, with millions of Americans tuning in on a daily basis. Now, with unemployment at an all-time high, more Americans than ever were relying upon radio to provide them with their evening's entertainment. In 1930, NBC began airing live Sunday broadcasts of the New York Philharmonic Orchestra with Arturo Toscanini conducting, while CBS inaugurated the country's first regular broadcasting schedule in 1931, beginning with a telecast featuring performances by George Gershwin, the Boswell Sisters, and Kate Smith. The company also gave **Bing Crosby** a fifteen-minute spot each evening; Crosby's soft croon, like that of Rudy Vallee (who hosted NBC's *The Fleischmann Hour*, the first radio variety show), was perfectly suited to the intimacy of the medium, and listeners showed their undying appreciation by sending a seemingly endless string of hits to the top of the pop charts.

But if radio proved invaluable to the careers of crooners like Crosby and Vallee, its emphasis on classical music and mainstream pop could be frustratingly limited, especially for listeners who couldn't afford a phonograph. **Jukeboxes** had been around since 1906, when inventor John Gabel first introduced his "Automatic Entertainer," but by the late 1930s, the jukebox industry was

positively booming. Most restaurants and bars (yes, bars; by 1933, Congress had finally given in to public pressure and repealed Prohibition) had a Wurlitzer, Seeburg, Mills, AMI, or Rock-Ola jukebox in the corner, and a mere nickel would get you several plays of your choice: something by Duke Ellington, the Mills Brothers, Fats Waller, or Ethel Waters, perhaps? Or maybe The Glenn Miller Band's "*In The Mood*," which, sixty years after its release, remains the quintessential artifact of the Swing Era.

Other popular personalities on 1930s radio included gossip columnist Walter Winchell, "singing cowboy" Gene Autry, vocalist Eddie Cantor, and a variety of comedic refugees from the vaudeville circuit, including Jack Benny, Fred Allen, the husband-and-wife team of George Burns and Gracie Allen, and the ventriloquist-and-dummy team of Edgar Bergen and Charlie McCarthy. Popular programs included *Little Orphan Annie*, *The Lone Ranger*, *Jack Armstrong, The All-American Boy*, *Fibber McGee and Molly*, and Bob Hope's *Pepsodent Show*. There was also **Father Charles Coughlan**, whose anti-Semitic rants were so virulent that CBS actually kicked him off the air. Undaunted, Father Coughlan set up his own radio network and found a receptive audience; in a mid-1930s poll, he was named the second most popular man in America—behind FDR, of course.

Perhaps the most notorious example of radio's hold over the public imagination was the evening of October 30, 1938, when Orson Welles staged a radio play of HG Wells' **The War of the Worlds** as part of his *Mercury Theater on the Air* program. Though disclaimers were aired at the beginning of the broadcast, many who tuned in later on became convinced that New Jersey was actually being attacked by Martian invaders. Within minutes, the radio station's phone lines were jammed by panicked listeners, and hundreds of others ran screaming from their homes before order could be sufficiently restored.

Lakehurst, New Jersey had been the site of a real disaster a year earlier, when the German zeppelin *Hindenburg* (left) exploded while attempting to land. The tragedy was broadcast over radio station WLS, which had sent announcer Herbert Morrison to cover the aircraft's arrival. Fifteen passengers, twenty crewmen, and one line-handler were killed in the conflagration, the cause of which has never truly been determined; in an era where measured, unemotional announcements were the radio norm, Morrison's hysterical reportage—"Oh, the humanity!"—struck a deep chord with the American public. Not surprisingly, the *Hindenburg* disaster effectively ended the brief vogue for lighter-than-air travel.

Unemployment dropped substantially during FDR's first term in office, and his Works Progress Administration projects (**WPA** for short) created hundreds of thousands of jobs across the country; many of the buildings, bridges, highways and murals commissioned by the WPA are still in existence. But the country's economic recovery proved sluggish, and the droughts (and subsequent dust storms) that ravaged the Midwest didn't help any. Like the characters in John Steinbeck's **The Grapes of Wrath**, many Midwestern farmers packed up their families and meager belongings and headed for California,

only to be met by billboards imploring them to go back where they came from. Maps and guidebooks to 1930s Los Angeles included the friendly message: "WARNING! While the attractions for tourists are unlimited, please advise anyone seeking employment not to come to Southern California, as natural attractions have already drawn so many capable, experienced people that the present demand is more than satisfied."

In truth, the American economy didn't truly pick up again until 1939, when the growing possibility of war with Germany initiated a substantial increase in US manufacturing. Relations between the two countries had been tense since 1933, when the American Federation of Labor had protested the Nazis' rise to power by calling for a boycott of all German-made products, but most Americans continued to hope that war was not in the offing. Indeed, several prominent Americans (like Henry Ford, himself the proud publisher of a bilious pamphlet entitled *The International Jew*) pushed for improved relations with Germany; when New York mayor Fiorello

LaGuardia announced that he wished his city's 1939–40 World's Fair had included a "chamber of horrors" with a Hitler room, many government officials demanded that the mayor make an apology.

Just the same, on September 16, 1940 Congress passed the **Selective Service Act**, which stipulated that nine hundred thousand American men between the ages of twenty and twenty-six would be drafted each year. Seven weeks later, FDR was re-elected for an unprecedented third term. Though his decision to run was controversial, most Americans seemed to feel that it was better not to "change captains in the middle of a storm"—and the storm clouds from the war in Europe seemed to be drifting closer by the moment.

War finally came on December 7, 1941, when Japanese forces launched a sneak attack on the US naval base at **Pearl Harbor**, Hawaii. Congress declared war against Japan the next day, and against Germany and Italy on December 11. With most able-bodied men pressed into military service, women joined the American work

force in record numbers. After Roosevelt instituted a minimum forty-eight-hour working week for war industries in labor-scarce areas, many black Americans moved from the South to the northern cities to find factory work, and farmers from the Midwest finally found themselves welcome in California.

In addition to the average Joes, the war effort snapped up most of the country's young film, radio, music, and athletics stars; some, like Glenn Miller, never came back. With most of their male objects of desire overseas, millions of young American women became fixated on a scrawny young singer named **Frank Sinatra**, who had been excused from the armed services because of a punctured eardrum. Though not the masterful interpreter he would later become, Sinatra did project an appealing vulnerability in songs like "All Or Nothing At All" and "You'll Never Know." Appealing to the ladies, that is; most American men, especially those serving in the military, openly resented the shrieks and swoons the singer elicited from "their" girls.

With rents and goods prices frozen to halt wartime inflation, the sale of new cars and trucks banned by the US Office of Production Management, and rationing ordered for sugar, coffee, rubber tires, gasoline, shoes, canned goods, meat, fat, and cheese, Americans on the home front suddenly found themselves with a surplus of cash, and with little to spend it on. As a result, nightclub and movie theater profits suddenly went through the roof.

From the dark days of the Depression, through the uncertainty of World War Two, Americans counted on **Hollywood** to distract them from

The inimitable Fred and Ginger.

their troubles and worries. Talking pictures, a novelty in the late 1920s, had quickly moved through their awkward, microphone-in-the-flower-pot adolescence. By the early 1930s, Hollywood understood that it took more than talking and singing actors to excite paying customers; over the next fifteen years, the studios responded by making hundreds of films that are still considered classics.

The 1930s and 1940s were something of a **golden age of film comedy**, with the Marx Brothers (*Duck Soup, A Night at the Opera*), WC Fields (*The Bank Dick, Never Give a Sucker an Even Break*), Mae West (*She Done Him Wrong, My Little Chickadee*), and Abbott and Costello (*Buck Privates, Rio Rita*) holding court as the top comedic stars of the day. Charlie Chaplin, who would eschew spoken dialogue until 1940's *The Great Dictator*, also produced two of his finest films— *City Lights* (1931) and *Modern Times* (1936)—during this period.

The horror film experienced an impressive revival, with audiences flocking to see Boris Karloff in *Frankenstein* (1931), *The Mummy* (1932), and *The Bride of Frankenstein* (1935); **Bela Lugosi** in *Dracula* (1931), *White Zombie* (1932), and *Island of Lost Souls* (1932); Fredric March in *Dr. Jekyll and Mr. Hyde*; an animated ape climb up New York's newly-erected Empire State Building in **King Kong** (1933); and Lon Chaney, Jr. in *The Wolf Man* (1941). And with gangsters like Al Capone and John

Dillinger still fresh in the public's memory, it was little wonder that films like *Little Caesar* (1931, with Edward G Robinson), *The Public Enemy* (1931, with James Cagney), and *Scarface: The Shame of the Nation* (1932, with Paul Muni) were so successful—or that a dapper actor named **Humphrey Bogart** would make a fortune playing tough guys in films like *The Petrified Forest* (1936), *The Maltese Falcon* (1941), and *Casablanca* (1943).

The period also produced a bumper crop of lavish musicals, including 1933's *42nd Street* and *Gold Diggers of 1933*, both of which were choreographed by the great Busby Berkeley. The same year saw **Fred Astaire and Ginger Rogers** paired for the first time in *Flying Down to Rio*; the coupling proved so popular that the

dancing duo appeared in nine subsequent films together, including *The Gay Divorcee* (1934), *Top Hat* (1935), *Swing Time* (1936), and *Shall We Dance?* (1937). Two other Rogers proved major draws: Will, the popular humorist who starred in several hits before his tragic death in a 1935 airplane crash; and Roy, who assumed the mantle of "top Western star" when Gene Autry joined the military.

Perhaps the two most successful (and enduring) musicals of the period were 1937's *Snow White and the Seven Dwarfs* and 1939's *The Wizard of Oz*. The former, the first feature-length

cartoon, was made by Walt Disney for a then-staggering 2.6 million dollars, while the latter featured several stunning color sequences, and made a star out of a young actress named Judy Garland. But the biggest stars of the era had to be **Shirley Temple** and **Clark Gable**. Not that they had much in common: Temple, a singing-and-dancing moppet with an excess of dimples and curls, was idolized by little girls for her roles in films like *Curly Top* (1935) and *Heidi* (1937); Gable, on the other hand, was idolized by men and lusted after by women. His role opposite Claudette Colbert in 1934's *It Happened One Night* made him a star, but it was his performance as Rhett Butler in 1939's epic *Gone With the Wind* that truly sealed his silver-screen immortality.

⬛ **Curly top herself: Shirley Temple.**

45

"With the world at peace," cheered a holiday advertisement for Firestone tires, "this Christmas will be the merriest in years." The Second World War had been a long, arduous, bloody, and dispiriting affair. As 1945 drew to a close, most Americans were ready to relax and have a good time. Wartime rationing of shoes, oil, meat, butter, and tires had recently been discontinued and "the boys" were starting to come home.

TRANS-LUX
PRESENTS
A
SPECIAL
V-J
DAY
PROGRAM

45 Celebrating the end of the war, a sailor kisses his girl.

However, from bedsheets to building materials, many goods were still scarce, and radio and print ads regularly reminded the public to continue buying war and **victory bonds** "to insure your splendid postwar world."

Despite creeping anxiety about the ramifications of the newly deployed atomic bomb, the postwar world did seem to offer some splendid possibilities. "Precooked frozen foods have a brilliant future," proclaimed *Consumer Reports* and, indeed, improved refrigeration technology was enabling consumers to store more foodstuffs, including frozen dinners. Heating them up was quite another matter, however. 1945 saw Percy LeBaron Spencer invent the **microwave oven**, but at three thousand dollars a pop, the Raytheon Company's new "Raydarange" was priced far out of the reach of most consumers.

45 Frozen foods were a boon for rationing-beset housewives.

US Signs Up For Austerity Drive

For the first time since 1941, Detroit's automobile factories began to roll out cars for civilian use; material shortages kept the assembly lines at a slow pace, however, and most folks looking to buy a new car had to sign up on a waiting list at their local dealer's showroom. General Motors hyped their "**Hydra-Matic Drive**—

the modern drive without a clutch pedal," while Ford boasted "more new developments than most prewar yearly models," but the truth was that most 1946 models did not differ appreciably from their 1942 counterparts; with the exception of minor alterations on the bumpers and radiator grille, Pontiac's 1946 **Silver Streak** sported virtually the same round-top design as the '42. The end of the year witnessed the introduction of Kaiser-Frazer's first cars. Though advertised as costing between twelve and fifteen hundred dollars (for the flashier Frazer) and a thousand dollars (for the more utilitarian Kaiser), the economical compacts hardly put a dent in the sales of Ford, General Motors or Chrysler-Plymouth, aka "The Big Three."

Radio Daze

After much discussion, the Federal Communications Commission decided to allocate thirteen channels for commercial television (Channel One was later reassigned for non-commercial

45 The Andrews Sisters, wartime favorites.

IN THE NEWS

February 4–11 – US President Franklin D Roosevelt, English Prime Minister Winston Churchill and Soviet leader Joseph Stalin attend top-secret Yalta Conference in the Ukraine; the discussion revolves around the postwar reorganization of Europe.

March 16 – Japanese island of Iwo Jima falls to US Marines.

April 12 – President Franklin D Roosevelt dies of cerebral hemorrhage; is succeeded by Vice-President Harry S Truman.

April 24 – First United Nations conference held in San Francisco, with delegates from 50 nations in attendance.

May 7 – Germany formally surrenders to Allied forces.

August 6 – Atom bomb dropped on Hiroshima.

August 9 – Atom bomb dropped on Nagasaki.

September 2 – Japan formally surrenders to Allied forces.

December 14 – John D Rockefeller donates $8.5 million for purchase of land along New York City's East River, to be used as a permanent headquarters by the fledgling United Nations.

use). As only roughly five thousand American homes actually had TV sets, most people continued to depend on radio for their home entertainment. Popular radio programs included the humorous **Red Skelton Show**, the action-packed serials *Green Hornet* and *Superman*, and the unbelievably maudlin *Queen for a Day*, a game show that awarded prizes to the female contestant with the most heartrending tale of woe.

Music News

"Rum And Coca-Cola," The Andrews Sisters' whitewashed rendition of a bawdy Trinidadian calypso number, was on everyone's lips, followed closely by Johnny Mercer's "On The Atchison, Topeka And Santa Fe" and Perry Como's "Till The End Of Time." Based on the melody from Frederic Chopin's "Polonaise In A Flat," Como's

hit capitalized on the **Chopin craze** then sweeping the country; thanks to Cornel Wilde's star turn in the Chopin biopic *A Song To Remember*, listeners both young and old were snapping up any Chopin records they could find.

Les Brown and His Orchestra scored big with "Sentimental Journey" and "My Dreams Are Getting Better All the Time" (both featuring vocals by a young Doris Day), and Vaughn Monroe

and His Orchestra had a huge hit with "There! I've Said It Again," but the era of the big bands was quickly coming to an end. Listeners were transferring their attentions and affections to solo vocalists such as Bing Crosby, Perry Como, Frank Sinatra, and Dinah Shore, as well as to rhythm 'n' blues combos like Louis Jordan and his Tympany Five ("Caldonia") and novelty acts like Spike Jones and His City Slickers ("Cocktails For Two"). Frustrated by the restrictions of big-band arrangements, many musicians found themselves drawn to the frantic improvisations of bebop, then currently being explored by trumpeter **Dizzy Gillespie** and saxophonist **Charlie Parker**. Without steady commercial prospects, the big bands proved too expensive to maintain; within a year, bandleaders Tommy Dorsey, Harry James, Woody Herman and Les Brown would all disband their orchestras.

Movie News

1945 was a landmark year for **Bing Crosby**. Not only did the mellow-voiced crooner rack up three Number One pop hits ("I Can't Begin To Tell You," "It's Been A Long, Long Time," and the perennial holiday favorite "White Christmas"), but the success of *Duffy's Tavern* and *The Bells of St Mary's* proved him the most popular male box-office attraction. He had plenty of competition from **Gregory Peck**, whose status as a Hollywood heartthrob was heightened by leading roles in *The Valley of Decision* (opposite **Greer Garson**, the top-drawing leading lady of 1945) and Alfred Hitchcock's *Spellbound* (opposite Ingrid Bergman, who didn't do too badly for herself in *Saratoga Trunk* and *The Bells of St Mary's*). John Wayne kept the world safe for democracy in *Back to Bataan* and *They Were Expendable*; meanwhile, on the home front, Joan Crawford won a Best Actress Oscar for her portrayal of a housewife-turned-waitress in *Mildred Pierce*.

Humphrey Bogart and Lauren Bacall, who played lovers in 1944's ***To Have and Have Not***, showed that their electric chemistry was not just an onscreen fluke; they married in 1945.

45 A boyish-looking Sinatra stood up for racial integration in 1945.

ACADEMY AWARDS

BEST PICTURE
....
The Lost Weekend
directed by Billy Wilder
....

BEST ACTOR
....
Ray Milland
The Lost Weekend
....

BEST ACTRESS
....
Joan Crawford
....
Mildred Pierce

45 Gregory Peck and Ingrid Bergman, spellbound by each other in Alfred Hitchcock's psychological mystery movie.

Life further imitated art in November, when Frank Sinatra, star of the recent Oscar-winning anti-racism short, *The House I Live In*, made a special appearance at a racial-tolerance rally in Gary, Indiana. White students at integrated Froebel High School had gone on strike against their new principal's "pro-Negro policies," which included letting black students join the orchestra and use the school pool. Between songs, "Ol' Blue Eyes" told the assembled students that racism was strictly for Nazis, and that if the Allied leaders could work out their differences, the kids of America could do the same.

Sounding a less optimistic note was **The Lost Weekend**, Billy Wilder's harrowing look at the life of a New York alcoholic, played by Ray Milland. Despite Paramount's uneasiness about releasing something so exceedingly bleak (much of the footage was actually shot in grimy New York City bars and the detox ward at Bellevue Hospital), the film took Best Picture honors, and Milland was awarded Best Actor. As Wilder told the *New York Times*, "If *To Have and Have Not* has established Lauren Bacall as The Look, then *The Lost Weekend* should certainly bring Mr Milland renown as The Kidney."

45 A stylish demonstration of Raytheon's electronic Raydarange.

As 1946 dawned, America woke up with a serious hangover.

The jubilant victory celebrations of late 1945 were over, pre-empted by the **dark uncertainties** of the postwar world. **The country was racked by spiraling inflation, labor disputes** involving over four million workers, **and a severe housing shortage.**

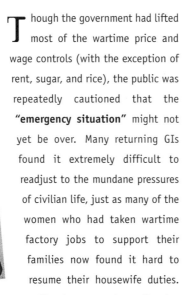

Though the government had lifted most of the wartime price and wage controls (with the exception of rent, sugar, and rice), the public was repeatedly cautioned that the **"emergency situation"** might not yet be over. Many returning GIs found it extremely difficult to readjust to the mundane pressures of civilian life, just as many of the women who had taken wartime factory jobs to support their families now found it hard to resume their housewife duties. From penthouse dinner parties to corner bars, Russian Communism and the atomic bomb were the main topics of conversation.

Movie News

No film better captured the uneasy mood of postwar America than William Wyler's **The Best Years of Our Lives**. The picture was an instant hit with American audiences, who saw their own hopes, fears, and travails reflected in the poignant story of three American vets returning home from World War Two. The film won seven Academy Awards, including Best Picture, Best Actor for Fredric March, and Best Supporting Actor for Harold Russell—an actual World War Two vet whose battle-mangled hands had been replaced with hooks. Best Actress went to Olivia de Havilland, for her performance in Mitchell Leisen's melodramatic *To Each His Own*. Failing to win anything at all was Frank Capra's **It's a Wonderful Life**, an uplifting, sentimental story of a depressed man who gets a second chance to straighten out his life. The Jimmy Stewart vehicle didn't even do much business at the box-office; in fact, it took several decades of televised screenings for the film to attain its present status as an American holiday classic.

Although Bing Crosby still reigned as the box-office king (thanks to *Road to Utopia* and *Blue Skies*), and Rita Hayworth's turn as the freewheeling *Gilda* established her as Hollywood's top sex symbol, Hollywood's 1946 output was decidedly less than frivolous. Ingrid Bergman, 1946's top female draw, spied on the Nazis with Cary Grant in Alfred Hitchcock's *Notorious*, and Tyrone Power and Gene Tierney pondered the meaning of life in Edmund Goulding's *The Razor's Edge*; but both films seemed like Walt Disney productions next to the cynical themes of such *films noir* as Howard Hawks' *The Big Sleep*, Tay Garnett's *The Postman Always Rings Twice*, Fritz Lang's *Scarlet Street,* and Otto Preminger's *Fallen Angel*. Such rampant pessimism did little to cloud **Norma Jeane Dougherty**'s skies, however; in August, 20th Century Fox signed the aspiring actress to a one hundred and twenty-five dollar a week contract, changing her name to **Marilyn Monroe** in the process.

July 1 – US atomic bomb tests held at Bikini Atoll in Pacific.

July 7 – Mother Francis Xavier Cabrini becomes the first American to be canonized by the Roman Catholic Church.

August 1 – Atomic Energy Commission created to promote peaceful application of atomic power.

Doin' What Comes Naturally

Show-business history was also being made in Atlantic City, New Jersey, where handsome crooner **Dean Martin** teamed up for the first time with pathologically goofy comedian **Jerry Lewis**, thus establishing a creative partnership that would make both of them rich and famous.

Across the state line, Irving Berlin's *Annie Get Your Gun*, starring Ethel Merman, was playing to sell-out crowds on Broadway. Perry Como's recording of the show's "They Say

It's Wonderful" and Dinah Shore's rendition of "Doin' What Comes Naturally" became huge chart hits, and Merman's showcase, "There's No Business Like Show Business," quickly entered the national consciousness.

Music News

Without question, the biggest song of the year was the Billy Reid composition **"The Gypsy."** Dinah Shore's recording of the song spent eight weeks at the top of the charts, whereupon it was promptly replaced by The Ink Spots' version—which, in turn, spent thirteen weeks at Number One. Other hits doing double duty at the top of the charts included Frankie Carle's "Oh! What It Seemed To Be," whose success was almost surpassed by Frank Sinatra's rendition, and the title song from *To Each His Own*, whose melody so captivated the American public that it hit Number One for no less than three artists (Eddy Howard and His Orchestra, Freddy Martin and

46 *Gilda*—a stylish and steamy Hollywood *film noir*.

His Orchestra, and The Ink Spots) and the Top Five for two others (Tony Martin, and The Modernaires with Paula Kelly).

Nat "King" Cole's Trio hit paydirt with the smooth "(I Love You) For Sentimental Reasons," and R&B superstar **Louis Jordan** continued to sell tons of records to black and white music lovers alike, hitting the pop charts four times ("Buzz Me," "Stone Cold Dead In The Market," "Choo Choo Ch'Boogie," and "Ain't That Just Like A Woman") over the course of the year. In the world of bebop, Dizzy Gillespie and Charlie Parker dissolved their partnership, after a two-month stand in Hollywood that puzzled audiences and critics as much as it excited their fellow musicians. Gillespie returned to New York City in February with the intention of organizing a bop orchestra, but Parker decided to stay in California. Unfortunately, Parker's precarious mental state (due, in part, to his raging heroin addiction) got the better of him; in July, he was committed to Camarillo State Hospital after accidentally starting a fire in his hotel.

Construction Goes On The Level

The postwar building boom going on across the nation was giving birth to a new kind of American dwelling: the "**ranch house**." The low-slung, single-story buildings were cheaper to build and to heat than the typical two-story-plus-attic house, and thus became immediately favored by a populace that was still experiencing the shortage of material goods. If it was still too costly to heat your ranch house, you could always spend your nights curled up under one of those new-fangled "electronic blankets," which the Simmons Company of Petersburg, Virginia, offered for $39.50 apiece.

Technology Starts To Count

American ingenuity, long directed towards the war effort, was now in full effect on the home front. The most interesting thing Detroit could come up with was a Nash 600 that could fit a double bed in its back seat, but things elsewhere were progressing rapidly. At the University of Pennsylvania, John P Eckert and John Mauchly developed the **ENIAC** (Electronic Numerical Integrator And Computer), the world's first electronic digital computer. The device required some eighteen thousand vacuum tubes, and so many components that they filled a 30- by 50-foot room; according to some witnesses, the ENIAC's initial power surge resulted in a brief brown-out throughout the city of Philadelphia.

...And Spring Arrives

The most momentous technological breakthrough, at least as far as American kids were concerned, was the invention of "**The Slinky**." Devised by marine engineer Richard James, the coiled spring that "walks up stairs,

46 Comedian Sammy Kaye tries out the brand new "Radio Chef," an electronic dime-in-the-slot frankfurter machine.

THE INK SPOTS

"The Gypsy"

FRANKIE CARLE AND HIS ORCHESTRA

"Oh! What It Seemed To Be"

FRANKIE CARLE AND HIS ORCHESTRA

"Rumors Are Flying"

EDDY HOWARD AND HIS ORCHESTRA

"To Each His Own"

DINAH SHORE

"The Gypsy"

alone or in pairs" became an immediate hit with the younger generation. Other offshoots, like "Slinky Dog" and "Cater-Puller," soon followed, but none of them ever matched the enormous success of the original item.

Time For A Fresh Look

Changes were afoot in the fashion world, as well; with the easing of wartime manufacturing restrictions, Americans now had a wider variety of clothes to choose from. The "slacks suits" popular with working women during the last years of the war were now out of favor, replaced by slim, belted dresses that rose to the knee. Also popular were dresses with shirtwaist tops, which buttoned all the way down the front. Colorful sports shirts were in for men, along with zipper-front casual jackets that could be worn with a shirt and tie.

46 The Inkspots—(*left to right*) Charles Fuqua, Bill Kenny, Herb Kenny, and Bill Bowen.

nineteen

Car designers began to look across the Atlantic for new ideas.

The 1948 model Lincoln Continental, Studebaker Coupe, and Hudson were all influenced by the **low, streamlined designs** currently coming out of France and England. Davis, an independent manufacturer, anticipated **consumer desire for smaller cars** with its bubble-shaped, three-wheeled vehicle.

47 Howard Hughes' *Spruce Goose* gets ready for takeoff in Los Angeles harbor.

The Davis could seat four persons on its single bench seat. Though it was priced at a reasonable $995, it was just too far ahead of its time to be successful. Also well ahead of its time was Cadillac; inspired by the Lockheed P-38 fighter plane, the company became the first to incorporate tailfins into its designs, putting them on all of their 1948 models. It would be several years, however, before the tailfin fad really caught on with American drivers.

Billed as "The first completely new car in fifty years," the Tucker, a six-passenger, four-door sedan, was the talk of the automobile world when it debuted in June of 1947. The car's rear-mounted, six-cylinder engine was made almost exclusively of aluminum, facilitating quick removal for repair purposes, and the front of the car sported three headlights, one of which would swivel to follow the curves of the road. "The car of the future" eschewed standard automobile parts like clutches, transmissions, differentials, and drive shafts, and the whole package was advertised at a little over a thousand dollars. There was only one catch: they weren't available yet. Despite selling millions of dollars worth of Tucker stock and franchises, Preston Tucker never seemed to have enough money to actually mass-produce his car. The Security Exchange Commission took a dim view of Tucker's dealings, and put him on trial for fraud. He was acquitted in 1949, but only fifty of his futuristic Tuckers were ever made. (The car and its inventor were eventually immortalized in Francis Ford Coppola's 1988 film, *Tucker: The Man and His Dream*.)

After a couple of years of treading water, the American automotive industry was finally starting to turn its eyes toward the future. In May, the BF Goodrich Tire Company introduced the tubeless tire, which was designed to seal itself when punctured. The **Harley-Davidson** company released its new **Panhead** motorcycle, featuring a redesigned Evolution engine. There were plenty of Harleys in attendance on July 4, when three thousand motorcycle enthusiasts rolled into Hollister, California, for a day of races. Fights with the local police quickly ensued, and the much-publicized incident, which indelibly molded the public's perception of the "outlaw" biker, later became the basis of the 1954 film *The Wild One*.

Set For Success

Commercial TV debuted in 1947; if it lacked much in the way of socially redeeming values—"It is a commercial reality but not yet an art," sniffed *Life* magazine—at least it was extremely entertaining. RCA marketed a small table television with a 6½- by 8½-inch screen, which sold for $325 plus a $55 "installation charge." Philco's 15- by 20-inch console model went for $795, plus

$85 installation, and Dumont's lavish Westminster emptied pocketbooks at $2,495, plus $75 installation. Most Americans, for the time being, did their TV watching in local taverns and bars, where the new invention was seen as a handy way to increase business.

Close Up And Dirty

Unsurprisingly, many of the year's more popular telecasts were of sporting events. Television exposure single-handedly resuscitated the popularity of **roller derby**, a brutal sport that essentially consisted of full-contact boxing on roller skates. Professional wrestling also reaped the benefits of the new medium; regular match broadcasts turned wrestler **"Gorgeous George" Wagner**—famous for wearing shocking pink shorts and his hair in a bleached-blond permanent wave—into one of the first television celebrities. At the peak of his popularity, he was earning seventy thousand dollars a year.

Major Breakthroughs

In September, the World Series of baseball was televised for the first time, although New York City, Washington, Philadelphia and Schenectady were the only cities to actually receive transmission. The seven-game contest between the New York Yankees and the Brooklyn Dodgers was notable for another reason: it featured the talents of Dodger **Jackie Robinson**, the first African-American player in the major

leagues. Despite constant abuse from fans and opposing players, Robinson kept his cool and played well enough to win "Rookie of the Year" honors, becoming an overnight folk hero in the process. Other black players who made the majors in 1947 were the Dodgers' Dan Bankhead, the Cleveland Indians' Larry Doby,

and Henry Thompson and Willard Brown of the St Louis Browns, but it would take until 1959 for the sport to be fully integrated.

Black Marx

Racial intolerance was also a hot issue in Hollywood, where Elia Kazan's *Gentleman's Agreement* (in which Gregory Peck pretends to be a Jew in order to understand how anti-Semitism

feels) was released against the protests of many studio heads, who worried that the film would draw undue attention to their own Jewishness.

They needn't have worried. As October's **House Committee on Un-American Activities** hearings indicated, the American government was much more concerned about "the extent of **Communist infiltration** in the Hollywood motion picture industry"

'47 *Left*: Jackie Robinson *Below*: Robinson signs autographs for young Dodgers fans.

than the influence of Jews. Called to testify before the committee, popular leading man Gary Cooper voiced the feelings of most of America, saying, "I never read Karl Marx, and therefore don't know so much about Communism except what I picked up from hearsay. But from what I heard I don't like it, because it's not on the level."

Starting To List

While many stars, writers, directors and studio heads testified before the committee that they were indeed fine, upstanding citizens, "**The Hollywood Ten**"—producer-director Herbert Biberman, director Edward Dmytryk, producer-writer Adrian Scott, and screenwriters Alvah Bessie, Lester Cole, Ring Lardner, Jr, John Howard Lawson, Albert Maltz,

Samuel Ornitz, and Dalton Trumbo—refused to divulge their political affiliations. Much to everyone's surprise, the ten men were convicted of contempt of Congress, and jailed for terms ranging up to a year. Wary of the specter of Communism, but even more frightened by the government probe, the film community effectively blacklisted the Hollywood Ten.

The Hollywood Committee for the First Amendment was formed in the fall by a group of Hollywood insiders (including Humphrey Bogart, Lauren Bacall, John Huston, Groucho Marx, Katharine Hepburn, Frank Sinatra, Fredric March, Gene Kelly, John Garfield, Ira Gershwin, and Danny Kaye) who claimed that, by forcing citizens to state their political views,

the government was violating their civil rights. Unfortunately, the group quickly splintered in the face of in-fighting and intense media pressure.

Movie News

While the paranoia of the time is certainly still palpable in the grimness of such *noir* offerings as Robert Rossen's *Body and Soul*, Henry Hathaway's *Kiss of Death* and Jacques Tourneur's *Out of the Past*, there was plenty of Hollywood sunshine to go around, as well. Bing Crosby, once again the leading male screen attraction, starred with Bob Hope and Dorothy Lamour in **Road to Rio**, one of the best of their six "Road" comedies, which featured musical numbers and comedic situations set in exotic locales. Betty

Latin percussion and poly-rhythms into the music of his big band. Country star Merle Travis began making appearances with a solid-body electric guitar, constructed especially for him by luthier Paul Bigsby. Few others were ever made, but Bigsby's baby anticipated the solid-body electric boom by a good three years. On the country and western charts, a young Alabamian by the name of **Hank Williams** scored his first big hit with "Move It On Over." The sound of the song was pure country, but the attitude was pure rock 'n' roll.

Method In His Mumbling

On Broadway, musicals *Finian's Rainbow* and *Brigadoon* opened to immediate raves. The big news of the theater season, however, was Tennessee Williams' *A Streetcar Named Desire*, and its dynamic lead, **Marlon Brando**. Although often criticized for "mumbling" his lines, Brando drew praise for his performance, heralding the eventual rise of the empathetic "method" school of acting.

Nylon Clings

In 1947, American consumers were again hit hard by the rising costs of food, clothing, rent and other necessities. Still, many women managed to scrape up enough cash to outfit themselves in **"the Dior Look"** (also known as "the New Look")—padded-hip, full-skirted fashions that were becoming increasingly popular. Men's suits stayed conservative, although many men brightened up their wardrobes with madras shirts or wide, colorful ties. Synthetic blends of rayon and polyester also saw a rise in popularity, as postwar Americans found themselves with less time to actually do their ironing.

Tract House Dreams

Inspired by the postwar housing shortage, **Levittown**, the US's first mass-produced tract housing project, was built in Island Trees, Long Island, by developer William Levitt. Architectural critics and sociologists attacked its sterility and lack of individuality, but many returning GIs and their wives found the pre-fabricated community attractive, not to mention affordable—Levittown's Cape Cod-style homes could be had for $6,990 apiece. With its expansive front lawns, wide streets and look-alike houses, Levittown became the model for America's new suburbia. Sales of rotary lawn mowers soon increased dramatically, and the modern American cult of lawn care was on its way.

And Nevada Nightmares

After a disastrous grand opening in late 1946, the **Flamingo Hotel**, the first "sophisticated" hotel on "the strip," reopened in Las Vegas. Financed by mobster Bugsy Siegel (who, thanks to an assassin's bullets, would not live to see the end of 1947), the hotel helped shift the desert city's image from vice-ridden gambling town to glamorous vacation hot-spot.

Grable, whose gorgeous gams adorned the wall of every self-respecting army barracks, livened up the screen (and the box office) with leads in *The Shocking Miss Pilgrim* and *Mother Wore Tights*. Natalie Wood warmed hearts as Kris Kringle's pal in *Miracle on 34th Street*, and cartoon characters Tweetie and Sylvester teamed up for the first time in Warner Brothers' Oscar-winning *Tweetie Pie*. Walt Disney mixed cartoon sequences with live action in **Song of the South**; while many have since derided the film as racist, it did provide the music industry with one of the year's most popular songs. Thanks to recorded versions by Johnny Mercer, Sammy Kaye, and The Modernaires with Paula Kelly, it was impossible to go anywhere without hearing "**Zip-a-Dee-Doo-Dah**."

Music News

In 1947, the most interesting musical developments were taking place off of the pop charts. In New York, **Dizzy Gillespie** introduced Afro-Cuban jazz to American listeners by incorporating

47 Marlon Brando (far left) smolders in the Broadway production of *A Streetcar Named Desire*.

48

"What time is it? Howdy Doody Time, of course!" Introduced during the last week of 1947, *The Howdy Doody Show* (originally titled Puppet Playhouse) quickly became required viewing for the youth of America. Hosted by "Buffalo Bob" Smith, and featuring occasional appearances from Clarabelle the Clown (aka Bob Keeshan, who later got his own children's TV gig as the titular host of Captain Kangaroo), the variety show's main draw was Howdy Doody, an inquisitive puppet with freckles and a plaid shirt.

The program took place in front of a live audience of children, known as "The Peanut Gallery." Savvy businessmen made millions from Howdy Doody dolls, records, toys, sleeping bags, wallpaper and wristwatches, convincing wary executives that television was indeed a profitable medium for advertising.

Popular from the get-go, TV was widely assailed as the eventual destroyer of American literacy, movies and theater. Although Ed Sullivan's *Toast of the Town* variety show (renamed **The Ed Sullivan Show** in 1955) lent the medium some class (well, just a touch of it—Sullivan's first broadcast did include singing fireman Fred Kohoman), the success of puppet shows like *Howdy Doody* and *Kukla, Fran and Ollie* didn't exactly reflect well upon its intellectual content.

What was most frightening, at least to the movie industry, was the obvious hold that television exerted over its viewers. Milton Berle's

48 The phenomenally successful Howdy Doody with Princess Summerfall Winterspring.

weekly comedy series, **The Texaco Star Theater**, was so popular that many restaurants would stay closed on Tuesday nights rather than compete; the show's October 19 broadcast earned a ninety-two-percent viewer share, still the highest rating ever. A former vaudevillian, Berle indulged in plenty of outrageous antics (including dressing up in women's clothing), but his real cultural contribution was the shot in the arm his show gave to the television industry—many Americans actually purchased their first TV sets just so they could watch "**Uncle Miltie**" in the privacy of their own homes.

Television wasn't the only threat facing the major film studios in 1948. The US Supreme Court ruled that Columbia, Metro-Goldwyn-Mayer, Paramount, RKO, 20th Century Fox, Warner Bros., and Universal would all have to divest themselves of their theater chains, effectively ending their monopoly over the exhibition of films. Thanks to competition from television, foreign filmmakers

48 Right from the start, television had an irresistible attraction for the American people.

(Hollywood bigwigs were less than thrilled by *Hamlet*'s Academy Awards success), and smaller companies like Republic and Monogram, the late forties and early fifties saw the majors pumping more and more money into lavish productions. As a result, they found it increasingly difficult to afford to keep large numbers of actors and directors under contract. By the end of the fifties, Hollywood's "studio system" had virtually collapsed, giving actors and directors a greater degree of independence and control over their own careers.

Movie News

But the main reason to go to a movie theater in 1948 was the sheer quality of the stuff being screened. Bing Crosby (*The Emperor Waltz*) and Betty Grable (*That Lady in Ermine*, *When My Baby Smiles at Me*) retained their top box-office status despite the fluffiness of their vehicles, but folks were also buying plenty of tickets to see Bogart in **The Treasure of the Sierra Madre** and *Key Largo*, Ingrid Bergman in *Joan of Arc*, and John Wayne in *Red River* and *Fort Apache*. Orson Welles' *The Lady from Shanghai* led the pack of excellent *noir* thrillers, including Rudolph Maté's *The Dark Past*, John Farrow's *The Big Clock*, and Anthony Mann's *Raw Deal*. Viewers who packed the theaters for *Rachel and the Stranger* didn't go for its pioneer-era

love story, but rather for the chance to gawk at **Robert Mitchum**. In a bizarre twist of fate, Mitchum's recent arrest for **marijuana** possession lent an added dose of reality to his "outsider" characters, and actually made him more popular at the box office.

Still struggling to make it in Hollywood, **Marilyn Monroe** appeared in bit roles in *Scudda-Hoo! Scudda-Hay!* and *Dangerous Years* before being dropped by 20th Century Fox. She then signed with Columbia, but was released soon after playing the lead in *Ladies of the Chorus*. Out of work and hungry, she posed nude for photos that would later see the light of day in the form of a million-selling calendar. Marilyn's modeling fee? Fifty dollars.

48 Aspiring young actress Marilyn Monroe.

Music News

1948's pop charts offered something for just about everyone, ranging from the comforting lilt of Bing Crosby's "Now Is The Hour (Maori Farewell Song)" and Nat "King" Cole's "Nature Boy," to the novelty charm of Art Mooney and His Orchestra's "I'm Looking Over a Four Leaf Clover," and Spike Jones and His City Slickers' crazed "All I Want For Christmas (Is My Two Front Teeth)". Rhythm 'n' blues continued to make its presence felt, most prominently in the form of Bull Moose Jackson and His Bearcats' "I Love You, Yes I Do" and The Orioles' "It's Too Soon to Know."

Thanks to the tireless efforts of Dizzy Gillespie, bebop was rising in popularity; many swing bands tried to incorporate bop into their repertoires, often with awkward results. Meanwhile, trumpeter Miles Davis formed a nine-piece **"Birth of the Cool"** combo (including baritone saxophonist Gerry Mulligan and alto saxophonist Lee Konitz), which utilized softer tones, a smoother rhythm section and more concise arrangements than bebop, pioneering "cool" jazz in the process.

In June, Columbia Records introduced their new 33⅓ rpm **"long-playing" record**. While the standard 78 rpm disc could only accommodate a maximum of four minutes of music, each side of Columbia's new album format could handle up to twenty-three, which made it ideal for classical selections. RCA also unveiled their new creation, the 7-inch 45 rpm disc. Originally intended for short classical pieces, the company quickly began using the format for pop singles.

Teenage The New Age

On December 20, *Life* magazine ran a cover story on **teenagers**, underscoring the fact that, for the first time in American history, teenagers were viewed as a demographic unto themselves. Thanks, in part, to the many extra jobs that were created by World War Two, teenagers had plenty of spending money, and it became Madison Avenue's avowed mission to get them to spend it on various clothing, dance and music fads.

1949 held more than its share of bad news for the United States. For the first time, the American Cancer Society and National Cancer Institute warned adult Americans (over forty percent of whom enjoyed at least a pack a day) that cigarette smoking might cause cancer. To make matters worse, the Soviet Union exploded its first atomic bomb. Stalin's government claimed that the bomb was detonated as a means of stimulating agricultural growth in a barren region of the USSR, but most Americans took it as a sign that a full-scale nuclear war was just around the corner.

TOP TV SHOWS

The Texaco Star Theater

The Toast of the Town

Arthur Godfrey's Talent Scouts

Fireball Fun for All

Philco Television Playhouse

ACADEMY AWARDS

BEST PICTURE

All the King's Men
directed by Robert Rossen

BEST ACTOR

Broderick Crawford
All the King's Men

BEST ACTRESS

Olivia de Havilland
The Heiress

Beginning a pattern that would continue, more or less unabated, through to the present day, Americans responded to the ominous global developments by zoning out in front of the television. By 1949, Americans were buying one hundred thousand TV sets a week. Critics noted a substantial increase in mystery and horror programming from the previous year, which was just fine with the viewers who tuned in regularly for gritty shows including *Lights Out*, *Man Against Crime* and *Hands of Murder*. **Captain Video**, featuring former radio actor Al Hodge, was American television's first science-fiction program; despite tremendously cheesy props and cardboard scenery, it gained a huge following. **The Lone Ranger**, based on the popular radio serial, also debuted in 1949, with Clayton Moore in the title role and Jay Silverheels as Tonto.

On a more wholesome note, **The Goldbergs**, based on a long-running radio sitcom, gave TV its first Jewish family. Though extremely popular with viewers, the hit show was dropped in 1951, when anti-Communist pamphlet *Red Channels* listed Phillip Loeb, who played Mr Goldberg, as "friendly to Communist causes." The show returned in 1952 with a different Mr Goldberg, but only lasted a few more years. Unable to find further work, the blacklisted Loeb killed himself in 1955.

Show Of Hands Leads To Emmy

Los Angeles' Hollywood Athletic Club hosted the first annual Emmy Awards ceremony, an event which was all but ignored by the news media. As a result, America missed the once-in-a-lifetime opportunity to see Shirley Dinsdale and her puppet, Judy Splinters, win the Emmy for Outstanding Personality.

Movie News

Betty Grable was still America's most popular leading lady, but even her star power (and legs) couldn't save *The Beautiful Blonde from Bashful Bend* from laying an egg at the box office. Grable's main competition was from **Esther Williams**, a great swimmer and serviceable actress who turned heads in *Take Me Out to the Ball Game* and *Neptune's Daughter*. John Wayne was undoubtedly the number one box-office draw in the country, putting in lead appearances in *Three Godfathers*, *The Fighting Kentuckian*, and *She Wore a Yellow Ribbon*. Errol Flynn, one of America's favorite male stars during World War Two, appeared in the title role of *The Adventures of Don Juan*, but the film did little to boost his sagging popularity.

Other popular films included Stanley Donen's musical **On the Town** (starring Gene Kelly and Frank Sinatra as swabbies on shore leave), the costume spectacle **Samson and Delilah** (with Victor Mature and Hedy Lamarr), and **Francis**, the first of several successful low-brow comedies starring Francis the Talking Mule. Just to show that it was on the right side of the anti-Communist cause, Hollywood produced three Red-bashing features, *The Red Menace*, *The Red Danube*, and *Guilty of Treason*. None of them did particularly well with filmgoers.

Two great entertainment duos made their film debuts in 1949: Dean Martin and Jerry Lewis in *My Friend Irma*, and the Roadrunner and Wile E Coyote in Chuck Jones' animated short, *Fast and Furryous*.

America's Driving Force

There were over thirty-four thousand miles of road improvements and construction carried out on American highways during 1949, and it was considered every citizen's patriotic duty to take advantage of them. In Detroit, the auto makers were gearing up for the coming decade with various improvements, both cosmetic and functional. Plymouth hailed its "Improved Air Pillow Ride" and "Safe-Guard Hydraulic Brakes," noting that its 1950 models were "Packed with value and ready to prove it!" 1950 Hudsons offered "the new step-down ride," with a lower center of gravity than any other American car, while ads for the 1950 Studebaker trumpeted its rocket-derived "Next Look." Flashiest of all were Oldsmobile's 88 and 98 models, both of which were part of Olds' new "Futuramic" line.

The postwar automobile culture also had a hand in shaping modern American architecture. In Los Angeles, John Lautner's design for **Googie's** coffee shop featured jaunty angles and

IN THE NEWS

Construction begins on UN Headquarters in New York City.

September 3 – Soviet Union explodes its first atom bomb.

October 21 – Judge Harold Medina sentences "eleven top US Communists" to prison terms of up to five years.

a dynamic exterior sign, both of which were created for the express purpose of attracting the attention of passing motorists. Once thought of as sleazy dives, coffee shops and diners were now considered respectable places for family dining, and Googie's comfortable spaces and bright color scheme virtually defined 1950s' coffeeshop architecture.

Music News

In 1949, music lovers could take advantage of the RCA's new 7-inch format with the Emerson 45 rpm record player, available at participating dealers for just $39.95. It's quite likely most folks who bought the Emerson player used it to listen to their new **Perry Como** singles. It was another stellar year for Como, who landed nine singles in the Top Twenty, including "Some Enchanted Evening", "Forever And Ever," and "Bali Ha'i"—the latter from the popular Rodgers and Hammerstein musical *South Pacific*, which was currently raking in the cash on Broadway. One of the year's biggest singles was Gene Autry's "**Rudolph The Red-Nosed Reindeer.**" Autry's recording of Johnny Marks' Christmas song sold over two million copies in the month of December, and became a Yuletide standard. Louis Jordan and

Ella Fitzgerald's "Baby, It's Cold Outside" wasn't a Christmas hit (it came out in June), but it should have been.

Refugees from the country charts, Hank Williams' "Lovesick Blues" and Ernest Tubb's "Slipping Around" both snuck into the pop Top 25, although the latter song would eventually top the pop charts in a duet version by Jimmy Wakely and Margaret Whiting. "Drinkin' Wine Spo-Dee-O-Dee," a crossover R&B hit for "Stick" McGhee, was the first in a long line of R&B and rock hits for New York's Atlantic label.

In November, Charlie Parker recorded a groundbreaking jazz session with a string section. "Bird," Parker's nickname, was immortalized a month later when the **Birdland** jazz club opened on Broadway in New York City.

49 Charlie Parker (second from right) and friends at Birdland.

TOP HITS

VAUGHN MONROE ORCHESTRA
"Riders In The Sky (A Cowboy Legend)"

FRANKIE LAINE
"That Lucky Old Sun"

EVELYN KNIGHT
"A Little Bird Told Me"

VIC DAMONE
"You're Breaking My Heart"

RUSS MORGAN AND HIS ORCHESTRA
"Cruising Down The River"

Pots Of Dough

Peter Hodgson, an unemployed ad copywriter, raised a few eyebrows when he placed a pink-looking compound of boric acid and silicone oil on the market. The compound had been invented during World War Two by General Electric engineer James Wright, but Wright could find no conceivable use for the stretchable, bounceable substance. Christened **Silly Putty**, Hodgson's product was an immediate hit with America's kids, who of course found innumerable uses for it. Priced at a dollar per one-ounce glob, Silly Putty eventually grossed Hodgson over a hundred and forty million dollars.

Index

Acknowledgements

The publishers would like to thank the following sources for their kind permission to reproduce the pictures in this book:

The Advertising Archives

Corbis-Bettmann/UPI

Ford

Ronald Grant Archive

The Image Bank/Archive Photos

The Robert Opie Collection

Pictorial Press Limited

Every effort has been made to acknowledge correctly and contact the source and/or copyright holder of each picture, and Carlton Books Limited apologises for any unintentional errors or omissions which will be corrected in future editions of this book.

About the Author

Dan Epstein is an award-winning freelance writer and editor who has contributed to many magazines. Since graduating in Film Studies from Vassar College in New York, he has worked for *Chicago Subnation*, a bi-monthly magazine devoted to the city's popular culture, and for the *Los Angeles Reader*. He has also had his work published in *Guitar Player*, *LA Weekly*, *Mojo*, and *Time Out Guide* to Los Angeles.